43 Roses

43 Roses

Poems for Lovers

compiled by

Mike Parker

WordCrafts

43 Roses
Copyright © 2017
Mike Parker

All poems are in the public domain. All rights reserved. No part of this publication may be reproduced, stored in a retrieval system, or transmitted in any form or by any means, electronic, mechanical, photocopying, recording, or otherwise, without written permission from the publisher.

Published by WordCrafts Classics
A division of WordCrafts Press
Buffalo, Wyoming 82834
www.wordcrafts.net

Contents

She Walks in Beauty 1
To Fanny Brawne 2
La Vita Nuova 3
Because She Would Ask Me Why 4
How Do I Love Thee 5
Life in a Love 6
A Red, Red Rose 8
Love and Friendship 9
I Loved You First: But Afterwards 10
That I Did Always Love 12
Sonnet 18 13
This Dream 14
Sonnet 116 15
If All Those Endearing Young Charms 16
The Indian Serenade 18
Evening Song 20
Beautiful Dreamer 21
One Day I Wrote Her Name 22
Who Will Save Me? 23
Sonnets from the Portuguese, 14 24
The Rose of Sharon 25
There is a Lady Sweet and Kind 26

Love's Philosophy	27
The Passionate Shepherd to His Love	28
Did Not	30
A White Blossom	31
The White Rose	32
Monna Innominata	33
To My Dear and Loving Husband	34
Meeting at Night	35
Lovers' Infiniteness	36
Valentine	38
Wild Nights-Wild Nights!	40
Roses	41
Love's Trinity	42
Love and Friendship	43
At Last	44
Longing	46
Again and Again	47
A Gift	48
El Beso	49
Rabbi Ben Ezra	50
Ode	54

For Paula

Grow old with me.
 The best is yet to be!

She Walks in Beauty
Lord Byron

She walks in beauty, like the night
Of cloudless climes and starry skies;
And all that's best of dark and bright
Meet in her aspect and her eyes;
Thus mellowed to that tender light
Which heaven to gaudy day denies.

One shade the more, one ray the less,
Had half impaired the nameless grace
Which waves in every raven tress,
Or softly lightens o'er her face;
Where thoughts serenely sweet express,
How pure, how dear their dwelling-place.

And on that cheek, and o'er that brow,
So soft, so calm, yet eloquent,
The smiles that win, the tints that glow,
But tell of days in goodness spent,
A mind at peace with all below,
A heart whose love is innocent!

To Fanny Brawne

John Keats

I cannot exist without you – I am forgetful of every thing but seeing you again – my life seems to stop there – I see no further. You have absorb'd me.

I have a sensation at the present moment as though I were dissolving …I have been astonished that men could die martyrs for religion – I have shudder'd at it – I shudder no more – I could be martyr'd for my religion – love is my religion – I could die for that – I could die for you.

My creed is love and you are its only tenet – you have ravish'd me away by a power I cannot resist.

La Vita Nuova

Dante Alighieri

In that book which is
My memory...
On the first page
That is the chapter when
I first met you
Appear the words...
Here begins a new life

Because She Would Ask Me Why I Loved Her

Christopher Brennan

If questioning would make us wise
No eyes would ever gaze in eyes;
If all our tale were told in speech
No mouths would wander each to each.

Were spirits free from mortalmesh
And love not bound in hearts of flesh
No aching breasts would yearn to meet
And find their ecstasy complete.

For who is there that lives and knows
The secret powers by which he grows?
Were knowledge all, what were our need
To thrill and faint and sweetly bleed?

Then seek not, sweet, the "If" and "Why"
I love you now until I die.
For I must love because I live
And life in me is what you give.

How Do I Love Thee
Elizabeth Barrett Browning

How do I love thee?
    Let me count the ways
I love thee to the depth
    and breadth and height
My soul can reach,
    when feeling out of sight.
For the ends of Being and ideal Grace
I love thee to the level of everyday's
Most quiet need, by sun and candlelight.
I love thee freely, as men strive for right
I love thee purely,
    as they turn from praise
I love thee with the passion put to use
In my old griefs,
    and with my childhood's faith.
I love thee with a love I seemed to lose
With my lost saints,
    –I love thee with the breath,
Smiles, tears, of all my life!
    — and, if God choose,
I shall but love thee better after death.

Life in a Love
Robert Browning

Escape me?
Never—
Beloved!
While I am I, and you are you,
So long as the world contains us both,
Me the loving and you the loth,
While the one eludes,
    must the other pursue.
My life is a fault at last, I fear—
It seems too much like a fate, indeed!
Though I do my best
    I shall scarce succeed—
But what if I fail of my purpose here?
It is but to keep the nerves at strain,
To dry one's eyes and laugh at a fall,
And baffled, get up to begin again,—
So the chase takes up one's life, that's all.
While, look but once
    from your farthest bound,
At me so deep in the dust and dark,
No sooner the old hope drops to ground

Than a new one,
    straight to the selfsame mark,
I shape me—
Ever
Removed!

A Red, Red Rose

Robert Burns

O my luve's like a red, red rose.
That's newly sprung in June;
O my luve's like a melodie
That's sweetly play'd in tune.

As fair art thou, my bonnie lass,
So deep in luve am I;
And I will love thee still, my Dear,
Till a'the seas gang dry.

Till a' the seas gang dry, my Dear,
And the rocks melt wi' the sun:
I will luve thee still, my Dear,
While the sands o'life shall run.

And fare thee weel my only Luve!
And fare thee weel a while!
And I will come again, my Luve,
Tho' it were ten thousand mile!

Love and Friendship
Emily Bronte

Love is like the wild rose-briar,
Friendship like the holly-tree—
The holly is dark when the rose-briar blooms
But which will bloom most constantly?

The wild rose-briar is sweet in spring,
Its summer blossoms scent the air;
Yet wait till winter comes again
And who will call the wild-briar fair?

Then scorn the silly rose-wreath now
And deck thee with the holly's sheen,
That when December blights thy brow
He still may leave thy garland green.

I Loved You First: But Afterwards

Christina Rossetti

Poca favilla gran fiamma seconda. - Dante

Ogni altra cosa, ogni pensier va fore,
E sol ivi con voi rimansi amore. - Petrarca

I loved you first: but afterwards your love
Outsoaring mine, sang such a loftier song
As drowned the friendly cooings of my dove.
Which owes the other most?

My love was long, And yours
    one moment seemed to wax more strong;
I loved and guessed at you,
    you construed me
And loved me
    for what might or might not be -

Nay, weights and measures
    do us both a wrong.
For verily love knows not 'mine' or 'thine;'
With separate 'I' and 'thou' free love has done,

For one is both and both are one in love:
Rich love knows nought of 'thine that is not mine;'
Both have the strength
    and both the length thereof,
Both of us,
    of the love which makes us one.

That I Did Always Love
Emily Dickenson

That I did always love
I bring thee Proof
That till I loved
I never lived—Enough—

That I shall love alway—
I argue thee
That love is life—
And life hath Immortality—

This—dost thou doubt—Sweet—
Then have I
Nothing to show
But Calvary—

Sonnet 18
William Shakespeare

Shall I compare thee to a summer's day?
Thou art more lovely and more temperate:
Rough winds do shake the darling buds of May,
And summer's lease hath all too short a date:
Sometime too hot the eye of heaven shines,
And often is his gold complexion dimm'd;
And every fair from fair sometime declines,
By chance,
    or nature's changing course, untrimm'd;
But thy eternal summer shall not fade
Nor lose possession of that fair thou ow'st;
Nor shall Death brag
    thou wander'st in his shade,
When in eternal lines to time thou grow'st;
So long as men can breathe or eyes can see,
So long lives this, and this gives life to thee.

This Dream

Edna St. Vincent Millay

Love, if I weep it will not matter,
    And if you laugh I shall not care;
Foolish am I to think about it,
    But it is good to feel you there.

Love, in my sleep I dreamed of waking,
    White and awful the moonlight reached
Over the floor, and somewhere, somewhere,
    There was a shutter loose, it screeched!

Swung in the wind, and no wind blowing!
    I was afraid, and turned to you,
Put out my hand to you for comfort,
    And you were gone! Cold, cold as dew,

Under my hand the moonlight lay!
    Love, if you laugh I shall not care,
But if I weep it will not matter,
    Ah, it is good to feel you there!

Sonnet 116

William Shakespeare

Let me not to the marriage of true minds
Admit impediments. Love is not love
Which alters when it alteration finds,
Or bends with the remover to remove:
O no! it is an ever-fixed mark
That looks on tempests and is never shaken;
It is the star to every wandering bark,
Whose worth's unknown,
    although his height be taken.
Love's not Time's fool,
    though rosy lips and cheeks
Within his bending sickle's compass come:
Love alters not
    with his brief hours and weeks,
But bears it out even to the edge of doom.
If this be error and upon me proved,
I never writ, nor no man ever loved.

If All Those Endearing Young Charms

Thomas Moore

Believe me,
    if all those endearing young charms,
Which I gaze on so fondly to-day,
Were to change by to-morrow,
    and fleet in my arms,
Live fairy-gifts fading away,
Thou wouldst still be adored,
    as this moment thou art,
Let thy loveliness fade as it will,
And around the dear ruin
    each wish of my heart
Would entwine itself verdantly still.

It is not while beauty and youth are thine own,
And thy cheeks unprofaned by a tear,
That the fervor
    and faith of a soul may be known,
To which time will but make thee more dear!
No, the heart that has truly loved
    never forgets,
But as truly loves on to the close,

As the sunflower
    turns on her god when he sets
The same look
    which she turned when he rose!

The Indian Serenade
Percy Bysshe Shelley

I arise from dreams of thee
    In the first sweet sleep or night,
When the winds are breathing low,
    And the stars are shining bright:
I arise from dreams of thee,
    And a spirit in my feet
Has led me- who knows how?
    To thy chamber-window, sweet!

The wandering airs they faint
    On the dark, the silent stream-
The champak odors fail
    Like sweet thoughts in a dream;
The nightingale's complaint,
    It dies upon her heart-
As I must die on thine,
    Oh, beloved as thou art!

Oh, lift me from the grass!
    I die! I faint! I fail!
Let thy love in kisses rain
    On my lips and eyelids pale.

My cheek is cold and white, alas!
    My heart beats loud and fast-
Oh! press it close to thine own again,
    Where it will break at last!

Evening Song
Sidney Lanier

Look off, dear Love, across the sallow sands,
And mark yon meeting of the sun and sea;
How long they kiss in sight of all the lands,
Ah! longer, longer we.

Now, in the sea's red vintage melts the sun
As Egypt's pearl dissolved in rosy wine
And Cleopatra-night drinks all- 'tis done,
Love, lay thine hand in mine.

Come forth, sweet stars,
    and comfort heaven's heart,
Glimmer, ye waves,
    'round else unlighted sands;
Oh night! divorce our sun and sky apart-
Never our lips, our hands.

Beautiful Dreamer
Stephen Foster

Beautiful dreamer, wake unto me,
Starlight and dewdrops are waiting for thee;
Sounds of the rude world heard in the day,
Lull'd by the moonlight have all pass'd a way!

Beautiful dreamer, queen of my song,
List while I woo thee with soft melody;
Gone are the cares of life's busy throng, --
Beautiful dreamer, awake unto me!

Beautiful dreamer, out on the sea
Mermaids are chaunting the wild lorelie;
Over the streamlet vapors are borne,
Waiting to fade at the bright coming morn.

Beautiful dreamer, beam on my heart,
E'en as the morn on the streamlet and sea;
Then will all clouds of sorrow depart, --
Beautiful dreamer, awake unto me!

One Day I Wrote Her Name

Edmund Spenser

One day I wrote her name upon the strand,
But came the waves and washed it away:
Again I wrote it with a second hand,
But came the tide
   and made my pains his prey.
"Vain man," said she, "that dost in vain essay
A mortal thing so to immortalize;
For I myself shall like to this decay,
And eke my name be wiped out likewise."
"Not so," quoth I; "let baser things devise
To lie in dust, but you shall live by fame;
My verse your virtues rare shall eternize,
And in the heavens write you glorious name:
Where, whenas Death
   shall all the world subdue,
Our love shall live, and later life renew."

Who Will Save Me?
Unknown (13th Century)

There are little traits that keep me bound...
I think of nothing else
    save the bright face of my lady-

Ah me!
Her swan-white throat, her strong chin,
Her fresh laughing mouth
    which daily seems to say,
"Come kiss me, love, kiss me once again!"

Her regal nose, her smiling grey eyes-
    (That thieves to steal a lover's heart)-
And her brown tresses that wildly fly.
Each have wounded me as with a dart

So amorous are these
    that I deem they will slay me.
Ah God, ah God!
Alas, who will save me?

Sonnets from the Portuguese, 14
Elizabeth Barrett Browning

If thou must love me, let it be for nought
Except for love's sake only.
Do not say;
'I love her for her smile, her look,
Her way of speaking gently,
For a trick of thought
That falls in well with mine,
and certes brought
A sense of pleasant ease on such a day.'

For these things in themselves, Beloved,
May Be changed,
Or change for thee,
And love, so wrought, may be unwrought so.
Neither love me for thine own dear pity's
Wiping my cheeks dry.
A creature might forget to weep,
Who bore thy comfort long,
And lose thy love, thereby!

But love me for love's sake, that evermore
Thou mayst love on, through love's eternity.

The Rose of Sharon
Solomon

I am the rose of Sharon,
and the lily of the valleys.
As the lily among thorns,
so is my love among the daughters.
As the apple tree among the trees of the wood,
so is my beloved among the sons.

I sat down under his shadow
    with great delight,
and his fruit was sweet to my taste.
He brought me to the banqueting house,
and his banner over me was love.
Stay me with flagons, comfort me with apples:
for I am sick of love.

His left hand is under my head,
and his right hand doth embrace me.
I charge you, O ye daughters of Jerusalem,
by the roes, and by the hinds of the field...
that ye stir not up, nor awake my love...
till he please.

There is a Lady Sweet and Kind

Thomas Ford

There is a lady sweet and kind,
Was never a face so pleased my mind;
I did but see her passing by,
And yet, I'll love her till I die.

Her gesture, motion, and her smiles,
Her wit, her voice my heart beguiles,
Beguiles my heart, I know not why,
And yet, I'll love her till I die.

Cupid is winged and he doth range,
Her country, so, my love doth change:
But change she earth, or change she sky,
Yet, I will love her till I die.

Love's Philosophy
Percy Bysshe Shelley

The fountains mingle with the river,
    And the rivers with the ocean;
The winds of heaven mix forever,
    With a sweet emotion;
Nothing in the world is single;
    All things by a law divine
In one another's being mingle;--
    Why not I with thine?

See the mountains kiss high heaven,
    And the waves clasp one another;
No sister flower would be forgiven,
    If it disdain'd its brother;
And the sunlight clasps the earth,
    And the moonbeams kiss the sea;--
What are all these kissings worth,
    If thou kiss not me?

The Passionate Shepherd to His Love

Christopher Marlowe

Come live with me and be my love,
And we will all the pleasures prove,
That valleys, groves, hills and fields,
Woods or steepy mountains yields.

And we will sit upon the rocks,
Seeing the shepherds feed their flocks
By shallow rivers, to whose falls
Melodious birds sing madrigals.

And I will make thee beds of roses,
And a thousand fragrant posies,
A cap of flowers and a kirtle
Embroidered all with leaves of myrtle;

A gown made of the finest wool,
Which from our pretty lambs we pull;
Fair-lined slippers for the cold,
With buckles of the purest gold;

A belt of straw and ivy buds,
With coral clasps and amber studs;
And if these pleasures may thee move,
Come live with me and be my love.

The shepherd swains shall dance and sing
For thy delight each May morning;
If these delights thy mind may move,
Then live with me and be my love

Did Not

Thomas Moore

Twas a new feeling--something more
Than we had dared to own before,
Which then we hit not;
We saw it in each other's eye,
And wished, it every half-breathed sigh,
To speak, but did not.

She felt my lips' impassioned touch-
Twas the first time I dared so much,
And yet she chid not;
But whispered o'er my burning brow,
"Oh, do you doubt I love you now?"
Sweet soul! I did not.

A White Blossom

DH Lawrence

A tiny moon as white and small
    as a single jasmine flower
Leans all alone above my window,
    on night's wintry bower,
Liquid as lime-tree blossom,
    soft as brilliant water or rain
She shines, the one white love of my youth,
    which all sin cannot stain.

The White Rose
John Boyle O'Reilly

The red rose whispers of passion,
And the white rose breathes of love;
O, the red rose is a falcon,
And the white rose is a dove.

But I send you a cream-white rosebud
With a flush on its petal tips;
For the love that is purest and sweetest
Has a kiss of desire on the lips.

Monna Innominata
(I wish I could remember)

Christina Rossetti

I wish I could remember that first day,
First hour, first moment of your meeting me,
If bright or dim the season, it might be
Summer or Winter for aught I can say;
So unrecorded did it slip away,
So blind was I to see and to foresee,
So dull to mark the budding of my tree
That would not blossom for many a May.
If only I could recollect it, such
A day of days! I let it come and go
As traceless as a thaw of bygone snow;
It seemed to mean so little, meant so much;
If only now I could recall that touch,
First touch of hand in hand-
    Did one but know!

To My Dear and Loving Husband

Anne Bradstreet

If ever two were one, then surely we.
If ever man were loved by wife, then thee;
If ever wife was happy in a man,
Compare with me ye women if you can.

I prize thy love more than whole mines of gold,
Or all the riches that the East doth hold.
My love is such that rivers cannot quench,
Nor ought but love from thee give recompense.

Thy love is such I can no way repay;
The heavens reward thee manifold, I pray.
Then while we live, in love let's so persever,
That when we live no more we may live ever.

Meeting at Night
Robert Browning

The gray sea and the long black land;
And the yellow half-moon large and low:
And the startled little waves that leap
In fiery ringlets from their sleep,
As I gain the cove with pushing prow,
And quench its speed i' the slushy sand.

Then a mile of warm sea-scented beach;
Three fields to cross till a farm appears;
A tap at the pane, the quick sharp scratch
And blue spurt of a lighted match,
And a voice less loud, through joys and fears,
Than the two hearts beating each to each!

Lovers' Infiniteness

John Donne

If yet I have not all the love,
Dear, I shall never have it all,
I cannot breathe one other sigh, to move,
Nor can entreat one other tear to fall.
All my treasure, which should purchase thee,
Sighs, tears, and oaths, and letters I have spent,
Yet no more can be due to me,
Than at the bargain made was meant.
If then thy gift of love were partial,
That some to me, some should to others fall,
    Dear, I shall never have thee all.

Or if then thou gavest me all,
All was but all, which thou hadst then;
But if in thy heart, since, there be or shall
New love created be, by other men,
Which have their stocks entire, and can in tears,
In sighs, in oaths, and letters outbid me,
This new love may beget new fears,
For, this love was not vowed by thee.
And yet it was, thy gift being general,
The ground, thy heart is mine; whatever shall
    Grow there, dear, I should have it all.

Yet I would not have all yet,
He that hath all can have no more,
And since my love doth every day admit
New growth,
    thou shouldst have new rewards in store;
Thou canst not every day give me thy heart,
If thou canst give it, then thou never gav'st it;
Love's riddles are, that though thy heart depart,
It stays at home, and thou with losing sav'st it:
But we will have a way more liberal,
Than changing hearts, to join them, so we shall
    Be one, and another's all.

Valentine

Elinor Wylie

Too high, too high to pluck
My heart shall swing.
A fruit no bee shall suck,
No wasp shall sting.

If on some night of cold
It falls to ground
In apple-leaves of gold
I'll wrap it round.

And I shall seal it up
With spice and salt,
In a carven silver cup,
In a deep vault.

Before my eyes are blind
And my lips mute,
I must eat core and rind
Of that same fruit.

Before my heart is dust
At the end of all,
Eat it I must, I must
Were it bitter gall.

But I shall keep it sweet
By some strange art;
Wild honey I shall eat
When I eat my heart.

O honey cool and chaste
As clover's breath!
Sweet Heaven I shall taste
Before my death.

Wild Nights – Wild Nights!

Emily Dickinson

Wild Nights – Wild Nights!
Were I with thee
Wild Nights should be
Our luxury!
Futile – the winds –
To a heart in port –
Done with the compass –
Done with the chart!
Rowing in Eden –
Ah, the sea!
Might I moor – Tonight –
In thee!

Roses

George Eliot

You love the roses - so do I. I wish
The sky would rain down roses, as they rain
From off the shaken bush. Why will it not?
Then all the valley would be pink and white
And soft to tread on. They would fall as light
As feathers, smelling sweet; and it would be
Like sleeping and like waking, all at once!

Love's Trinity

Alfred Austin

Soul, heart, and body, we thus singly name,
Are not in love divisible and distinct,
But each with each inseparably link'd.
One is not honour, and the other shame,
But burn as closely fused as fuel, heat, and flame.
They do not love who give the body and keep
The heart ungiven; nor they who yield the soul,
And guard the body. Love doth give the whole;
Its range being high as heaven, as ocean deep,
Wide as the realms of air
    or planet's curving sweep.

Love and Friendship
Emily Bronte

Love is like the wild rose-briar,
Friendship like the holly-tree—
The holly is dark when the rose-briar blooms
But which will bloom most constantly?

The wild rose-briar is sweet in spring,
Its summer blossoms scent the air;
Yet wait till winter comes again
And who will call the wild-briar fair?

Then scorn the silly rose-wreath now
And deck thee with the holly's sheen,
That when December blights thy brow
He still may leave thy garland green.

At Last

Elizabeth Akers Allen

At last, when all the summer shine
That warmed life's early hours is past,
Your loving fingers seek for mine
And hold them close—at last—at last!
Not oft the robin comes to build
Its nest upon the leafless bough
By autumn robbed, by winter chilled,—
But you, dear heart, you love me now.

Though there are shadows on my brow
And furrows on my cheek, in truth,—
The marks where Time's remorseless plough
Broke up the blooming sward of Youth,—
Though fled is every girlish grace
Might win or hold a lover's vow,
Despite my sad and faded face,
And darkened heart, you love me now!

I count no more my wasted tears;
They left no echo of their fall;
I mourn no more my lonesome years;
This blessed hour atones for all.
I fear not all that Time or Fate
May bring to burden heart or brow,—
Strong in the love that came so late,
Our souls shall keep it always now!

Longing
Matthew Arnold

Come to me in my dreams, and then
By day I shall be well again.
For then the night will more than pay
The hopeless longing of the day.

Come, as thou cam'st a thousand times,
A messenger from radiant climes,
And smile on thy new world, and be
As kind to others as to me.

Or, as thou never cam'st in sooth,
Come now, and let me dream it truth.
And part my hair, and kiss my brow,
And say My love! why sufferest thou?

Come to me in my dreams, and then
By day I shall be well again.
For then the night will more than pay
The hopeless longing of the day.

Again and Again
Rainer Maria Rilke

Again and again,
    even though we know love's landscape
and the little churchyard
    with its lamenting names
and the terrible reticent gorge
    in which the others end:
Again and again
    the two of us walk out together
under the ancient trees,
    lay ourselves down again and again
among the flowers,
    and look up into the sky.

A Gift

Amy Lowell

See! I give myself to you, Beloved!
My words are little jars
For you to take and put upon a shelf.
Their shapes are quaint and beautiful,
And they have many pleasant colours and lusters
To recommend them.
Also the scent from them fills the room
With sweetness of flowers and crushed grasses.
When I shall have given you the last one,
You will have the whole of me,
But I shall be dead.

El Beso

Angelina Weld Grimké

Twilight—and you
Quiet—the stars;
Snare of the shine of your teeth,
Your provocative laughter,
The gloom of your hair;
Lure of you, eye and lip;
Yearning, yearning,
Languor, surrender;
Your mouth,
And madness, madness,
Tremulous, breathless, flaming,
The space of a sigh;
Then awakening—remembrance,
Pain, regret—your sobbing;
And again, quiet—the stars,
Twilight—and you.

Rabbi Ben Ezra
Robert Browning

Grow old with me!
The best is yet to be,
The last of life, for which the first was made:
Our times are in His hand
Who saith "A whole I planned,
Youth shows but half; trust God:
    see all, nor be afraid!"

Not that, amassing flowers,
Youth sighed "Which rose make ours,
Which lily leave and then as best recall?"
Not that, admiring stars,
It yearned "Nor Jove, nor Mars;
Mine be some figured flame which blends,
    transcends them all!"

Not for such hopes and fears
Annulling youth's brief years,
Do I remonstrate: folly wide the mark!
Rather I prize the doubt
Low kinds exist without,
Finished and finite clods,
    untroubled by a spark.

I summon age
To grant youth's heritage,
Life's struggle having so far reached its term:
Thence shall I pass, approved
A man, for aye removed
From the developed brute;
    a god though in the germ.

And I shall thereupon
Take rest, ere I be gone
Once more on my adventure brave and new:
Fearless and unperplexed,
When I wage battle next,
What weapons to select,
    what armour to indue.

Youth ended, I shall try
My gain or loss thereby;
Leave the fire ashes, what survives is gold:
And I shall weigh the same,
Give life its praise or blame:
Young, all lay in dispute;
    I shall know, being old.

Note that Potter's wheel,

That metaphor! and feel
Why time spins fast, why passive lies our clay,—
Thou, to whom fools propound,
When the wine makes its round,
"Since life fleets, all is change; the Past gone,
    seize to-day!"

Fool! All that is, at all,
Lasts ever, past recall;
Earth changes, but thy soul and God stand sure:
What entered into thee,
That was, is, and shall be:
Time's wheel runs back or stops:
    Potter and clay endure.

Look not thou down but up!
To uses of a cup,
The festal board, lamp's flash and trumpet's peal,
The new wine's foaming flow,
The Master's lips a-glow!
Thou, heaven's consummate cup,
    what need'st thou with earth's wheel?

But I need, now as then,

Thee, God, who mouldest men;
And since, not even while the whirl was worst,
Did I,—to the wheel of life
With shapes and colours rife,
Bound dizzily,—mistake my end,
    to slake Thy thirst:

So, take and use Thy work:
Amend what flaws may lurk,
What strain o' the stuff,
    what warpings past the aim!
My times be in Thy hand!
Perfect the cup as planned!
Let age approve of youth,
    and death complete the same!

Ode

Arthur O'Shaughnessy

We are the music-makers,
And we are the dreamers of dreams,
Wandering by lone sea-breakers
And sitting by desolate streams;
World losers and world forsakers,
On whom the pale moon gleams:
Yet we are the movers and shakers
Of the world for ever, it seems.

With wonderful deathless ditties
We build up the world's great cities.
And out of a fabulous story
We fashion an empire's glory:
One man with a dream, at pleasure,
Shall go forth and conquer a crown;
And three with a new song's measure
Can trample an empire down.

We, in the ages lying
In the buried past of the earth,
Built Nineveh with our sighing,
And Babel itself with our mirth;
And o'erthrew them with prophesying
To the old of the new world's worth;
For each age is a dream that is dying,
Or one that is coming to birth.

Also Available From

WordCrafts Press

Illuminations
by Paula K. Parker

Maggie's Song
by Marcia Ware

You've Got It, Baby!
by Carmichael

Morning Mist
by Barbie Loflin

What the Dog Said
by Joanne Brokaw

www.wordcrafts.net

www.ingramcontent.com/pod-product-compliance
Lightning Source LLC
Chambersburg PA
CBHW022229010526
44113CB00033B/781